C000217652

A TIME TO DANCE

A TIME TO DANCE

PHOTOGRAPHS
ANN HENRICK

WORDS
MAEVE BINCHY

NEW
ISLAND

A TIME TO DANCE
First published 2006
by New Island
2 Brookside
Dundrum Road
Dublin 14
www.newisland.ie

ISBN 1 905494 32 7

Design by New Island
Printed in Spain by Castuera

NEW ISLAND ACKNOWLEDGE THE GENEROUS SUPPORT OF
IRISH LIFE CORPORATE BUSINESS FOR THE PUBLICATION OF THIS BOOK.

Irish Life

10 9 8 7 6 5 4 3 2 1

To my brothers John, Dan and Mike, and their families,
with all my love
AH

To dear Gordon Snell,
in the hope that we will grow very old
very happily together
MB

INTRODUCTION

Someone once said that I was over-celebratory. It was not said in praise but I took it as the greatest compliment on earth. How wonderful to be able to see something to celebrate in almost any situation and at any time of life! I bless and thank my good-tempered parents for giving me happy genes and for fate or fortune for making my path in life a fairly easy one.

I have had such *fun* everywhere and none of that has changed as I got older. There was the wonderful discovery that if you don't stop laughing and enjoying things in your fifties and sixties then it's unlikely that you will do so later on.

I have the feeling that Being Old is not going to be a huge problem. It's just another stage along the way. Everything else has been so satisfying so far there's no reason why the rest of it won't be fine too. Of course there will be things I can't do, but then don't we want different things at different times.

When I was twelve I used to hope I would find half a crown which would pay for endless rounds in the bumpers at the amusements in Ballybunion. When I was sixteen I would sit for hours planning my long, happy life as Marlon Brando's wife, which would begin as soon as he met me. Which he never did, so somehow it never happened.

In my early twenties I spent happy months studying the *ABC Shipping Guide of the World* and finding great ways to sleep on the decks of boats going to far away places.

When I was in my late twenties I always travelled with a change of clothes and my passport just in case there might be a job in Brussels or Strasbourg that day and the newspaper would send whoever was ready to leave. And sometimes it worked and I would find myself hurtling through the airport clutching my portable typewriter, thinking I was the bees' knees.

How I would *hate* to be doing any of those things now! And how very good it is not to be even remotely wistful for the long lost years of youth.

I never think back regretfully wishing for the good old days – the good days are now. We are a much more tolerant people and less hypocritical than we were fifty years ago. There is much more awareness of fairness and justice in our world than there used to be.

Nowadays I rejoice in the shorthand of friendships that have gone on for decades where we all know each other and share not only memories but hopes and plans as well. With the added bonus that we are not afraid to tell each other how much it means to share a sunny afternoon in the garden, or a hopeless game of cards where everyone forgets what was dealt, called or played.

Nowadays we don't hold back in telling our families that we love them. Once upon a time it was considered soppy, sentimental and deeply suspect. Back then people were forever regretting that they hadn't said it in time rather than waiting to say it at the funeral. That it's different now has to be a great change for the better.

I don't see Old Age as a lonely, empty time, I see it as a time full of family and friends, and a lot of laughter. All of which makes me delighted to welcome this new collection of pictures by my friend, Ann Henrick.

This is a joyful celebration of positive ageing and I found it heartwarming to turn the pages and see the faces full of experience, memories, life and hope. More than any number of words could possibly achieve these happy pictures deliver a sense of optimism and love of life that would make anyone look forward to getting older.

Every line on every face tells a story. This, reassuringly, is far from a make-over book where people struggle with plastic surgery, lasers and creams to erase the signs of living from their lives. The people in this book don't glory in letting themselves go, but neither are they obsessed with trying to remove the signs of character and normal chronological ageing by presenting a bland, featureless canvas. A face afraid to laugh or to show any emotion for fear of cracking the artificial surface is a face without interest. But a face that has been on many a journey, has opened eyes to everything that life offers and dreamed dreams will always be a face we can look at with pleasure. And this book is full of them.

No longer will we feel that age is a problem, a worrying situation, or an absence of glorious youth. It's just another time of our life, a time to laugh, a time to sing. A time to dance.

A time to tell others some of the wisdom we *must* have picked up along the way, unless we were asleep.

So I have spent a happy year listening to older people talk. I write things down in my notebook and I think about them. I have heard little to make me depressed but a lot to make me cheerful. The quotes I give are from the people that I listened to over twelve months, not the actual people pictured here. I just matched my notes to the pictures; they are not the words of the men and women photographed for this book.

I congratulate Ann Henrick for seeing so much to inspire and touch us in the faces she has photographed. She has done very well indeed to have recognised such spirit and to share the people she met, both well known and not so well known.

She tells me that she would not have been able to meet a lot of these wonderful people without the help of Teresa Killeen of the Clareville Centre, Glasnevin, and of Grace Maguire, Richard Grey and John Fallon of Dublin City Council.

We are all grateful to Age Action Ireland for their support and help and for all they do to help reinforce the many positive aspects of ageing

My congratulations too to the publishers, New Island, who are many, many years younger than the subjects of this book but who have already learned a similar wisdom and understanding about the love of life.

And to the generous sponsors, Irish Life Corporate Business, who have kindly helped in this book's publication.

But mainly I want to thank those who look out at us from these pages. The men and women smiling at us and telling us that if life is good then a long life is even better. They tell us that if we love life when we are young we will go on loving it. What better message can they bring us?

Maeve Binchy
Dublin, September 2006

WORK AND PLAY

There's a lot to be said for being older. They let you be a bit different, they give you more rope somehow. They're pleased to see you laughing rather than complaining. Nobody asks you to take that smirk off your face.

Years and years ago I had this pal. He came round to the house one day with his swimming trunks in his pocket. I asked, 'Why would we get into that cold water?' And he said, 'Why not?' And you know there was no good answer! We've been swimming for decades; it wakes us up, keeps us alert.

It makes me feel like a kid again. I sometimes feel that my mother is going to say, 'Come in out of that icy water, you'll catch your death of cold.' My mother? Lord, she would be over 100 now if she were alive.

Basically, all it is is getting cold for a little bit and then getting out and warming up again. Isn't the sea there for all of us? It would be bad mannered not to use it.

A great lesson for getting older, or any age really: When someone says, 'How are you?' you must regard it as a greeting, not a question. They don't want to know how you are. They would hate to hear any of the details. 'Fine as a young trout,' is a very suitable answer.

It's a great thing to have an interest. Getting older holds no terrors if you are always reading something, studying something, learning more. Nobody says now that you have reached this age or that and you must close down your mind.

If you've had an interesting life and seen and done a lot of things, it will show on your face.

'For me, life at 80 is much like life was at 25. I am lucky to be doing the same things I did then, but with more insight and experience.'
Garret FitzGerald

FUN

There are ways of coping with things, and you can either look on crutches and wheelchairs as signs of weakness or you can get a laugh out of them and be a bit unexpected. Unexpected is good, I think.

I love the way young people lower their voices or get embarrassed if sex is mentioned in front of us. I have to remember to try to look a bit shocked and bewildered. Otherwise the world tilts over for them. As I suppose it would have for me years back too.

Of course we were interested in sex and love and excitement. It just wasn't as obvious then I suppose, or so easily available. Lord, they have great fun nowadays without anyone raising an eyebrow. That's the only difference.

DRESSING UP

I used to be a bit anxious about all that dressing up and fancy dress when I was young. I thought you were meant to look terrific. Now I know it's much better to look funny, it makes people laugh and that's what it's about. All those years I wasted trying to look like a fairy princess, which was never really on the cards!

You're not so self-conscious when you've been around for a while. You don't mind dressing up as a cowboy or a belly dancer or a Roman soldier. It's not as if you're admitting some foolish dream or that it's saying anything about you that you don't want people to know.

'It is a common assumption that older people are great writers. The expectation is that they reminisce about times gone by. The truth is that older people have a lot to say about the here and now, as well as having dreams about the future.'
Michael D. Higgins

MUSIC AND ART

Happiness is making music, and the longer you have been playing the more pleasure you give and receive. A piano or an accordion does not know or care the age of whoever plays it. But the envy of the skill of playing music is still the same at 80 as it is at 18. We would all love to be able to do it.

DANCE

When I was a girl you had to be asked up to dance. Otherwise you sat there for the night. It was torture sitting there when the music was beating out and your whole body wanted to dance. Later it got better so that young people could just go and dance on their own and have a great night. It wasn't a series of possible rejections all night if you didn't look as pretty as some. Nowadays I've forgotten all the sitting out and I only remember swooping around the floor, so there must have been a lot of dancing when you think back on it.

We girls used to love the dance. I don't think the fellows cared about dancing at all, it was sort of a means to an end, if you know what I mean. Later, if they had you up for a few smoochy dances then you'd have to give them the going home. So now all that sort of thing is out of the way we girls love having a dance any time someone puts the music on!

'A wildlife filmmaker doesn't stop working until he falls off his perch.'
Éamon de Buitléar

FACES

Wouldn't it be great if you could see just one picture of the person you think you love as an old person? Just one snap and you'd know for certain if this was a person you could go through life with. You could read it in the lines on their face. But we don't see so we have to take a chance, all of us. I suppose that's what makes it all such a big adventure.

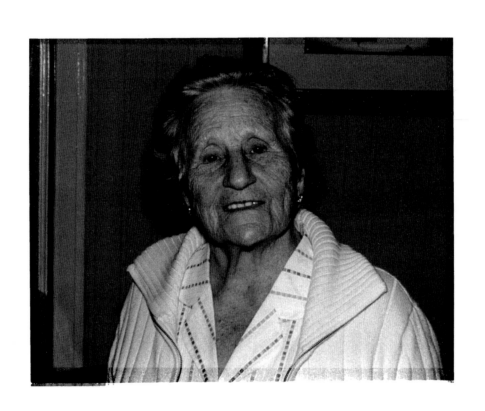

The odd thing is that when I go to the cinema these days all the young people look the same to me. It's not that I'm stupid – I can follow a plot with the best of them – but the hero and the villain and the detective and the lawyer and the neighbour all look exactly the same to me. They have the same hairstyle and the same outfits. Now with the older people it's easy; their lives are written on their faces and it's not hard to tell who is who and what has happened.

When I was at school I could tell you the people who were going to be happy and good-natured all their lives, no matter what was in store for them. When I see those people now I can still see their faces back in the classroom all those years ago. There were a few gloomy ones who got cheerful in later life, but the interesting thing is that the happy ones rarely ever got sour, so that must say something.

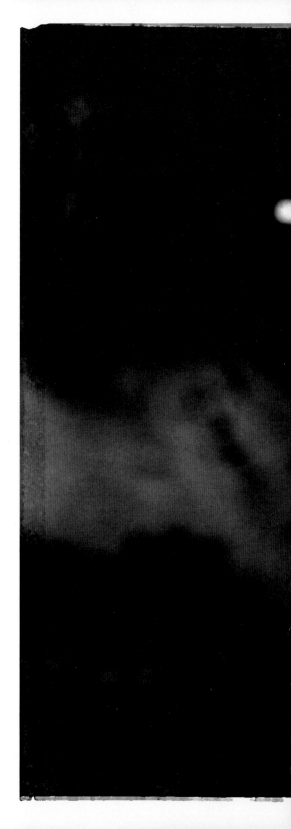

The lines on my mother's face were due to all the smiling to cheer us up when times were bad, and all the worrying when we weren't around to see her frowning over the debts and the poor future that seemed to lie ahead. Each line is there for us, her children who did so well. She once said that she wished she didn't look so wrinkled and maybe she let us down. For the first time in our lives we were totally speechless. We loved every single line on her face. They were a sign that we existed and had been greatly loved.

There are things you can see in a face and one of them is a sense of expectation. Happiness can be anywhere, like in the face of an older woman getting her hair done who knows she will look terrific when the styling is finished.

When I hear people wishing they were young again I don't join in. Well yes, I wish there was more time ahead I suppose, but I'm perfectly fine the way I am, knowing what I know instead of wondering and worrying.

'One has a wonderful view of the world from a bicycle.'
Dervla Murphy

FRIENDSHIP

You can get through any old thing
as long as you have a friend.

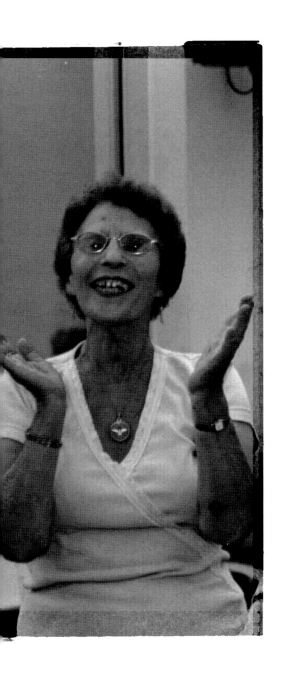

I think that I honestly know everything about my friend, every single detail of things she wouldn't tell her mother, her husband or her children. And she knows everything about me. It's like as if we don't even have to speak the words after all these years. We never asked each other to keep things a secret; we didn't have to! I'd trust her with my life. It's such an ease being with someone like that. I've told her not to fall off the perch because I'd be lost without her to talk to every day.

When you look at men they don't talk that much, do they? But they can still be great friends all the same. It's as if talking about work or sport or politics is a kind of code. They don't talk about emotional things or feelings from what I gather, yet my husband has a few friends and they'd die for each other. It's not friendship as we know it, but it's very powerful in its own way.

I am really sorry for anyone who doesn't have a friend, it must be a lonely, empty day without anyone to have a laugh with.

People don't know what a friend a pet can be. You can say completely unreasonable things to your dog or cat, but if you say them in a nice loving tone the animal will purr or wag its tail and be delighted with you. No wonder they are the best friends in the world!

Of course dogs aren't human – they are much, much better. They just know without being told when we don't feel great and need to be cheered up and when we want to be left in peace. Tell me how many humans know that?

You could tell a friend anything. Even that you were seriously going to murder your old fellow because he is so difficult, and the friend would say you were totally right but why not have a pot of tea or a small vodka instead for the moment and do it properly when the right time comes. And then years later the friend could say wasn't it as well we didn't murder your man, and you'd both have a great laugh over it.

'Mrs Kenny misses nothing.'
Maureen Kenny

COUPLES

I know the world is full of stories of doom and gloom in marriages but when you think of it isn't it amazing that people so often find exactly the right person to be their partner for life? It's such a leap in the dark, isn't it, signing on for ever with someone else. And no escape clauses in our day!

Growing up together and growing old together has been such an adventure. I know I have someone to come home to who will understand if the whole day has gone wrong. That's better than having millions in the bank.

I look at couples with a sort of wistfulness and I think to myself, 'Imagine all the secrets those two have shared.' And the couples have little ways of looking at each other that tell a whole story.

There was a quote I heard when I was young and single - 'He travels fastest who travels alone.' Fine, but is that what we want, to travel faster? I don't think so. And if you haven't had a travelling companion then who do you turn to when you want to share the memories?

There's a kind of peaceful feel about couples who have known each other for a long time and are happy. It doesn't matter if they finish each others' sentences, or they interrupt each other or contradict what the other says. They are two halves of a unit.

Isn't that what all the great love songs and love stories are about, a love that will last forever and ever? No wonder it's a pleasure to see a couple secure in what they have and have had for a long, long time. It makes sense of the world.

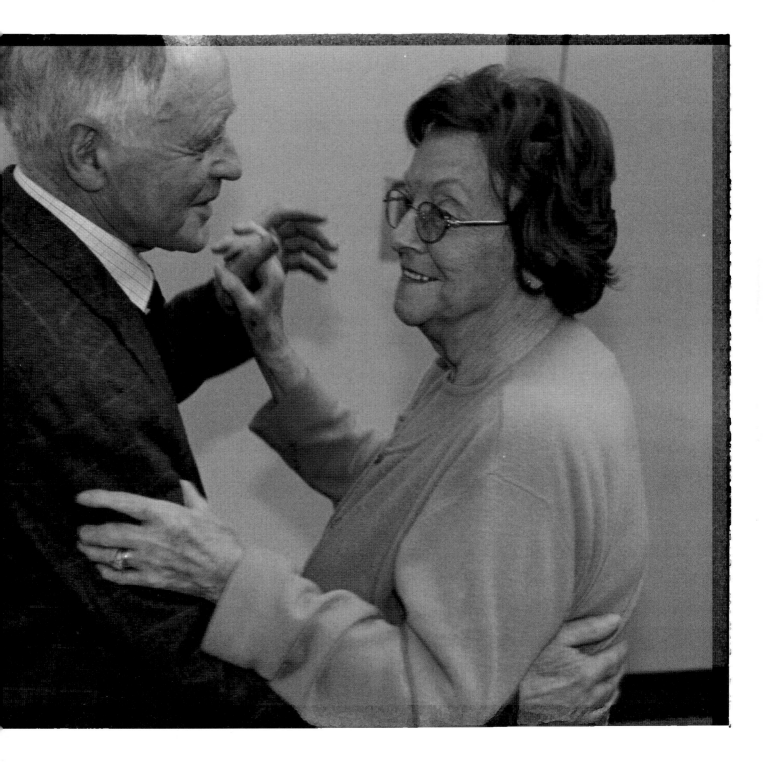

'Young people are attracted to the vitality they see in some older people.'
Pauline Bewick

FAMILY

Getting older is somehow like getting comfortable. I find a lot less stress in life these days and there's much more pleasure in simple things that I used to take for granted.

Age is not problem, a worrying situation, or an absence of glorious youth. It's just another time of our life, a time to laugh, a time to sing. A time to dance.